PLANETARY
EXPLORATION

MERCURY

HEATHER MOORE NIVER

Britannica®
Educational Publishing

IN ASSOCIATION WITH

ROSEN
EDUCATIONAL SERVICES

Published in 2017 by Britannica Educational Publishing (a trademark of Encyclopædia Britannica, Inc.) in association with The Rosen Publishing Group, Inc.
29 East 21st Street, New York, NY 10010

Distributed exclusively by Rosen Publishing.
To see additional Britannica Educational Publishing titles, go to rosenpublishing.com.

First Edition

Britannica Educational Publishing
J.E. Luebering: Executive Director, Core Editorial
Mary Rose McCudden: Editor, Britannica Student Encyclopedia

Rosen Publishing
Meredith Day: Editor
Nelson Sá: Art Director
Michael Moy: Designer
Cindy Reiman: Photography Manager
Bruce Donnola: Photo Researcher

Library of Congress Cataloging-in-Publication Data

Names: Niver, Heather Moore, author.
Title: Mercury / Heather Moore Niver.
Description: First edition. | New York : Britannica Educational Publishing in association with Rosen Educational Services, 2017. | Series: Planetary exploration | Includes bibliographical references and index.
Identifiers: LCCN 2016020474 | ISBN 9781508103738 (library bound) | ISBN 9781508104094 (pbk.) | ISBN 9781508103035 (6-pack)
Subjects: LCSH: Project Mariner (U.S.)—Juvenile literature. | Space flight to Mercury—Juvenile literature. | Mercury (Planet)—Exploration—Juvenile literature.
Classification: LCC QB611 .M58 2017 | DDC 523.41—dc23
LC record available at https://lccn.loc.gov/2016020474

Manufactured in China

Photo credits: Cover mr.Timmi/Shutterstock.com (Mercury); cover and interior pages background suns07butterfly/Shutterstock.com; pp. 4, 7, 15, 25, 26, 27 NASA/Johns Hopkins University Applied Physics Laboratory/Carnegie Institution of Washington; p. 5 Jamie Cooper/SSPL/Getty Images; p. 6, 24, 29 Science Source; p. 8 John Devolle/Ikon Images/Getty Images; p. 9 © Tristan3D/Alamy Stock Photo; p. 10 Jon Lomberg/Science Source; p. 11 Nicolle Rager Fuller/National Science Foundation; p. 12 NASA; pp. 13, 19 Stocktrek Images/Getty Images; p. 14 NASA/Duberstein; p. 16 Lyhne KRT/Newscom; p. 17 Gary Hincks/Science Source; p. 18 Mark Garlick/Science Source; p. 20 DEA Picture Library/De Agostini/Getty Images; p. 21 Bill Saxton, NRAO/AUI/NSF; p. 22, 23 NASA/JPL; p. 28 European Space Agency/Pierre Carril/Science Source.

CONTENTS

MEET A MORNING STAR

Mercury is one of the eight planets that orbit, or travel around, the sun in the solar system. It is the closest planet to the sun, which has made it a huge challenge for scientists to study. Its average distance from the sun is about 36 million miles (58 million kilometers). It travels around the sun at a faster speed than any other planet.

This image of Mercury was captured by a camera aboard the MESSENGER spacecraft.

THINK ABOUT IT

Mercury is mentioned in myths and stories in cultures around the world. It was named after the Roman god Mercury, the swift-footed messenger of the gods. Why might the planet have been named after this god?

Because Mercury is so close to the sun, the best time to see it from Earth is at sunrise or sunset. Mercury is known as a "morning star" at certain times of the year when it appears in the sky just before sunrise. At other times it appears as an "evening star" just after sunset.

Dawn is one of the best times to view Mercury, which is also called a "morning star."

Mercury

TAKE A LOOK AT MERCURY

Mercury is the smallest planet of the solar system. It is less than half the size of Earth. In fact, it would take eighteen Mercurys to fill up the inside of the Earth. Mercury is so small that it is smaller than some planets' moons! Mercury's diameter, or distance through its center, is about 3,030 miles (4,900 km). It is as wide as Earth's Atlantic Ocean.

Mercury's landscape includes flat

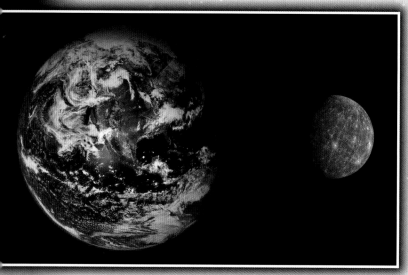

Mercury is not even half the size of Earth. In fact, Mercury is the solar system's smallest planet.

plains and long, steep cliffs. Pits called craters scar its surface. The craters form when chunks of rock or metal called meteorites hit Mercury. Some parts of the surface have many craters, while other parts are very smooth. The surface of Mercury does not have any water.

Like Earth, Mercury has three separate layers: a metallic core, a rocky **mantle**, and a thin rocky crust.

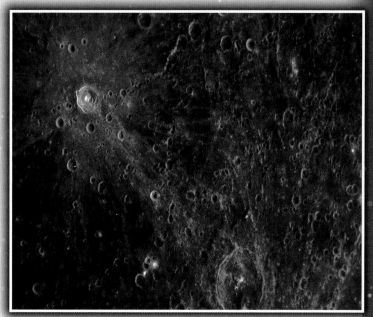

Meteorites crash into Mercury's surface and form craters, as seen in this photograph taken on January 14, 2008.

ROCKIN' PLANETS

P lanets are large natural objects that orbit, or travel around, stars. Eight planets orbit the star called the sun. In order from the closest to the sun, these planets are Mercury, Venus, Earth, Mars, Jupiter, Saturn, Uranus, and Neptune. The solar system is the collection of the sun and the objects that orbit around it, including the eight planets.

There are two main types of planets

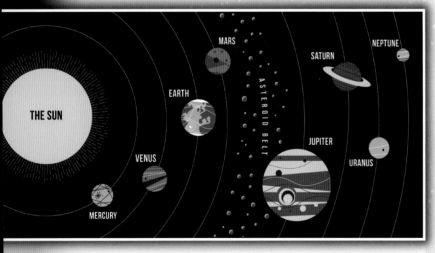

THE SUN

MERCURY

VENUS

EARTH

MARS

ASTEROID BELT

JUPITER

SATURN

URANUS

NEPTUNE

Eight planets orbit the sun. Jupiter, Saturn, Uranus, and Neptune are gas giants. Mercury, Venus, Earth, and Mars are rocky planets.

in the solar system: gaseous planets and rocky planets. Jupiter, Saturn, Uranus, and Neptune are called gas giants. They are made up mostly of gases and have no solid surfaces. The four planets nearest the sun—Mercury, Venus, Earth, and Mars—are called inner planets. They are rocky planets about the size of Earth or somewhat smaller.

Of all the planets, Mercury is the smallest and the densest, or most compact. It has the oldest surface and wild variations in surface temperature. It is also the least explored of the eight planets.

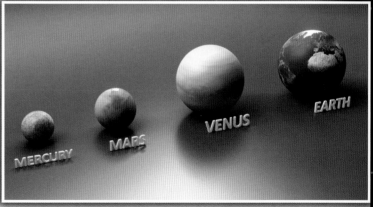

Mercury is the smallest of all the inner planets. The four rocky planets all have solid surfaces, like Earth.

HOW MERCURY WAS MADE

Mercury's position near the sun makes it tough to research how this rocky, iron-rich planet originally came to be a part of our solar system. However, scientists think that the sun and all of the planets formed from a gaseous cloud called a nebula. They think that the **elements** and dust from the nebula formed bodies that eventually came together to form the larger bodies of the solar system. Because Mercury is rich

Early stages of rotating cloud of gas and dust

Rotating cloud flattens as it contracts

Planets form within flattened cloud

The sun may have formed when dust and elements came together in a spinning nebula. As the nebula flattened, the sun and planets were formed.

in iron, scientists think that Mercury may have formed from the bodies that were a part of the inner solar system, where more iron would have been.

Another idea is that Mercury was involved in a gigantic collision. This space crash might have removed most of its outer layers. This might explain why so much of Mercury is made up of its core.

Mercury has a large core, which is rich with iron.

HOW MERCURY SHRANK!

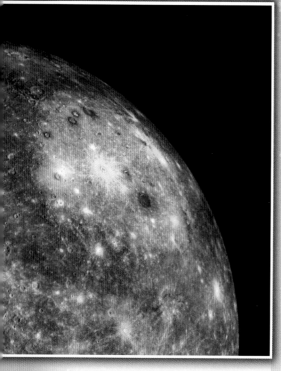

The Caloris basin is marked in yellow. The orange areas around the basin's edge may be volcanic vents.

Asteroids and meteorites constantly hit Mercury. They are always changing the planet's surface. One of the most notable structures on Mercury's surface is called the Caloris basin. The Caloris basin is especially big. It is about 800 miles (1,300 km) across. It was created when an asteroid crashed into Mercury's surface. This happened soon after the solar system was created.

Right after Mercury formed, it started to cool off. And as it cooled,

Mercury's crust is a thin, solid shell of rock. Earth's crust consists of separate plates of rock that move around. Compare how the surfaces of these two planets might have changed over time.

it shrank about 0.6 to 1.2 miles (1 to 2 km) over the next 500 million years. In some places, Mercury has lost more than 4 miles (7 km) in diameter since it was first formed. Its outer crust contracted and became so strong that even hot liquid rock called magma bubbling up from its core could not break through it.

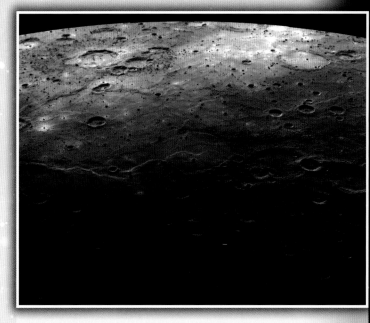

Similar to the surface of Earth's moon, Mercury's surface is covered in craters.

NO ATMOSPHERE: EXPLORE THE EXOSPHERE

A thin atmosphere called an exosphere surrounds Mercury. It does not keep in heat well, partly because winds from the sun blow the atmosphere away. Gases escape into space because the planet doesn't have much gravity.

Mercury's lack of atmosphere also means the planet experiences enormous temperature changes. An atmosphere would help keep heat in at night. As it is, Mercury's

SOLAR WIND

The sun's winds blow toward Mercury and blow heat and gases away since there isn't much gravity on Mercury.

Venus is the second planet from the sun. Though it is farther from the sun than Mercury is, Venus is hotter. What might cause Venus to be hotter than Mercury?

daytime temperatures are around 800°F (430°C). Overnight, temperatures drop to around −300°F (−180°C) just before dawn.

Asteroids often hit Mercury. So its surface is covered with craters, much like the moon. If Mercury had a thicker atmosphere, like Earth's, most asteroids would burn up before hitting the planet's surface. If Mercury had more gravity, like Earth, the planet would be able to keep a thicker atmosphere in place.

This image shows a double-ringed crater on Mercury in the bottom left. The crater might be filled with lava.

MERCURY'S UNUSUAL ORBIT AND SPIN

Like all planets, Mercury has two types of motion: orbit and spin. Mercury orbits, or travels around, the sun very quickly. It orbits at an average rate of about 30 miles (48 km) per second. Mercury completes one orbit around the sun every eighty-eight Earth days.

Mercury's short, uneven orbit takes it 29 million miles (47 million km) from the sun at its closest point and 43 million miles (70 million km) at its farthest point.

SUN

MERCURY

Like all the planets, Mercury travels around the sun in an oval-shaped orbit. However, Mercury's orbit has the longest oval shape of all the planets. How might the shape of a planet's orbit affect a planet?

In other words, one year on Mercury lasts eighty-eight Earth days. Mercury orbits around the sun so fast that people used to think it had to be two different planets!

Mercury's wild orbit takes it on a crazy path. It may travel as close as 29 million miles (47 million km) to the sun. At other times it can be far as 43 million miles (70 million km) away from the sun.

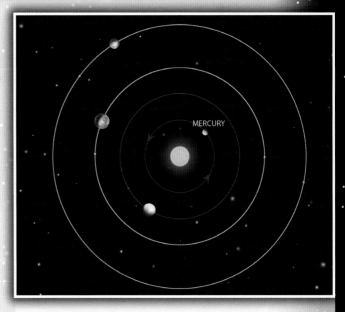

Like all the planets, Mercury orbits around the sun in a counter-clockwise direction.

A single day on Mercury lasts about 176 Earth days. These long days mean night and day have extremely different temperatures.

Although it has a speedy orbit, Mercury spins very slowly. The planet takes nearly fifty-nine Earth days to rotate once around its center.

This combination of a fast orbit and a slow spin leads to an unusual situation. A day on Mercury—the time it takes for the sun to appear straight overhead, to set, and then to rise straight overhead again—

If you were standing on Mercury when the planet is closest to the sun, the sun would appear more than three times as large as it would if you were standing on Earth. Why do you think it looks different on Mercury?

lasts about 176 Earth days. So on Mercury a "day" is longer than a "year." The long day on Mercury is another reason that the planet experiences an extreme difference in temperature from night to day.

When the sun comes up on Mercury, the temperature immediately begins to rise dramatically.

DISCOVERING MERCURY

People have known about Mercury for at least five thousand years. There is evidence that the Sumerian people wrote about it around 3000 BCE.

For hundreds of years scientists thought that Mercury and the other planets moved around Earth. Finally an astronomer named Nicolaus Copernicus changed that idea. He correctly stated that Earth and the other planets travel around the sun. His idea explained why Mercury and Venus always appear to be near the sun. Copernicus published his ideas in a book in 1543.

The ancient Sumerian people had their own astrological calendar.

For hundreds of years, most scholars believed that the sun, stars, and planets revolved around Earth. Why do you think they believed Earth was the center of the universe?

Mercury's closeness to the sun makes it difficult to observe from Earth. Instruments such as the Hubble Space Telescope and others are too sensitive to be pointed that close to the sun. Astronomers have used radar to study Mercury. They send radio waves toward the planet and detect and measure the waves that bounce back.

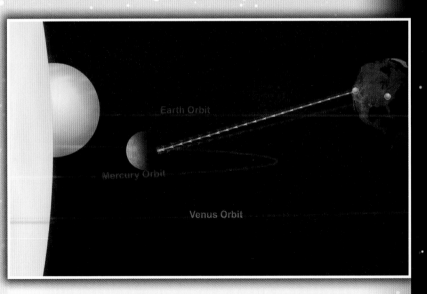

Mercury is difficult to observe, but scientists have learned about the planet by sending and receiving radio waves.

MARINER 10

Much of the first information known about Mercury came from Mariner 10. Mariner 10 was the first spacecraft to visit the planet. It was an unmanned spacecraft developed by the National Aeronautics and Space Administration (NASA) in the United States.

Mariner 10 launched on November 3, 1973. It first reached and flew by Mercury in March 1974. It later flew by

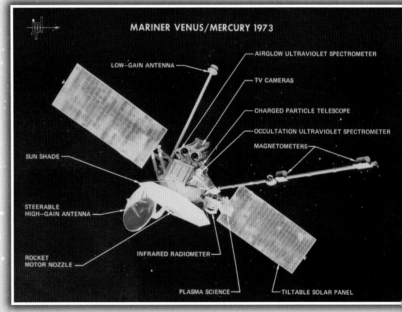

MARINER VENUS/MERCURY 1973

LOW–GAIN ANTENNA

AIRGLOW ULTRAVIOLET SPECTROMETER

TV CAMERAS

CHARGED PARTICLE TELESCOPE

OCCULTATION ULTRAVIOLET SPECTROMETER

MAGNETOMETERS

SUN SHADE

STEERABLE HIGH–GAIN ANTENNA

ROCKET MOTOR NOZZLE

INFRARED RADIOMETER

PLASMA SCIENCE

TILTABLE SOLAR PANEL

Mariner 10 was the first spacecraft that ever visited Mercury. The information it collected told scientists a lot about the mysterious planet.

the planet twice more. Data that Mariner 10 sent back to Earth answered a lot of questions about the planet Mercury. It also created questions, such as whether there was volcanic activity on the planet.

Mariner 10 was able to observe Mercury's surface, physical features, and atmosphere. It measured Mercury's wide range of temperatures. Mariner 10 also took photographs of almost half of the planet's surface. These photographs showed how similar Mercury's surface is to the surface of Earth's moon.

This photo mosaic of Mercury was taken by the Mariner 10 spacecraft in 1974.

MESSENGER TO MERCURY

MESSENGER launched on August 3, 2004. This trip found evidence that suggested the planet could have ice.

The United States sent a second unmanned craft, called MESSENGER, to Mercury in 2004. MESSENGER stands for MErcury Surface, Space ENvironment, GEochemistry, and Ranging mission. It launched from Cape Canaveral, Florida, on August 3, 2004.

MESSENGER first flew by Mercury on January 14, 2008. It made a second pass on October 6 later that same year. In 2011 it went into orbit around the planet. From its orbit it sent back photos of surfaces of

Mercury that no one had ever seen before.

Scientists had many questions about Mercury. One question was about ice. Earlier radar evidence had shown "radar-bright" spots that were thought to be ice. MESSENGER found evidence that areas around Mercury's poles were always in shadow, which would provide conditions for ice. More data from the spacecraft showed the presence of ice near Mercury's north pole.

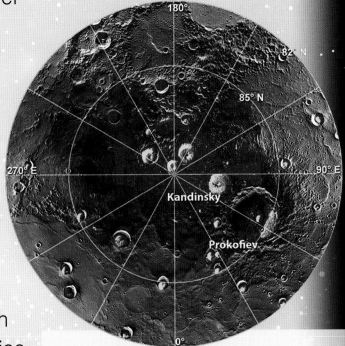

MESSENGER's trip to Mercury found evidence that the red areas shown in this image are always in shadow and that the yellow areas are ice.

MESSENGER's mission was supposed to last only until 2012. But NASA scientists were learning more about Mercury than ever! The special instruments on the **probe** gathered extremely detailed information. The scientists decided to let MESSENGER stay in space a while longer.

In 2012, MESSENGER delivered evidence that Mercury's core most likely makes up about 85 percent of its radius. (Earth's core makes up 50 percent of its radius.) The probe also showed that Mercury's surface is fairly smooth. It does not have many hills, compared to Mars or Earth's moon.

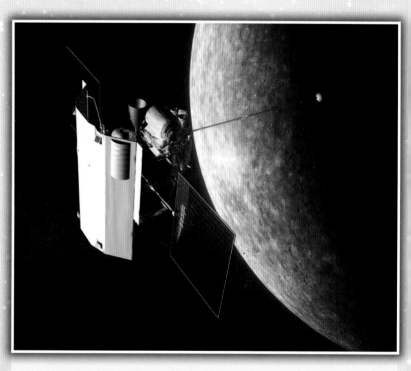

This is an artist's impression of the MESSENGER spacecraft at the planet Mercury.

MESSENGER could not stay in space forever. It eventually ran out of fuel. The spacecraft crashed into Mercury on April 30, 2015. The collision probably created a hole about 52 feet (16 meters) wide. The crash was expected.

MESSENGER took this image of the surface of Mercury during its mission to the planet. It crashed so hard into Mercury's surface that it probably left a new crater where it hit.

LEARNING MORE ABOUT MERCURY

The crash of MESSENGER was a disappointment, but more discoveries are definitely in store. Another exploration is in the works. Scientists in Europe and Japan worked together to build a probe called the BepiColombo Mercury probe. If all goes as planned, BepiColombo Mercury will travel to Mercury and orbit around the planet by 2024. The BepiColombo team plan to find the crater caused by the MESSENGER crash in 2015. Knowing the exact date

The BepiColombo Mercury probe should orbit Mercury by 2024 and locate the site of the MESSENGER crash.

In November 2015, it was reported that a comet known as Comet Encke was regularly showering Mercury with bits of dust. Given that Mercury's atmosphere is so thin, how might this affect the planet over time?

of the crash will help them study the rate of Mercury's space weathering, or surface changes caused by the planet's atmosphere and climate.

Mysterious Mercury seems like it will keep at least some of its secrets for a little while longer. But scientists will never give up trying to learn more about it.

An ancient comet called Comet Encke leaves dust in its path and showers Mercury with meteorites.

GLOSSARY

ASTEROID A small rocky body that moves around the sun. Many asteroids are found between the orbits of Mars and Jupiter.

ATMOSPHERE The gases that surround Earth, another planet, or a star.

COMET An object in outer space made primarily of ice and dust that develops a long, bright tail when it passes near the sun.

CONTRACTED Squeezed together so as to make smaller or shorter.

COOPERATIVE Willing to cooperate, or work together.

CRUST The rocky outer part of a planet, moon, or asteroid.

DIAMETER A straight line passing through the center of a figure or body, such as a circle or a sphere.

EVIDENCE Visible proof or a sign that something is true.

EXOSPHERE The outermost region of the atmosphere of a planet, or a thin layer of gases surrounding a body that has no other atmosphere.

GRAVITY A pulling force between bodies that exists on Earth and in space.

MAGMA Melted rock material within a planet.

METEORITE A chunk of rock or metal from space that hits a planet's surface.

ORBIT To move around another body.

PLAINS A broad area of flat land with few or no trees.

SOLAR SYSTEM A star with the group of bodies that revolve around it, especially the sun with the planets, moons, and asteroids that orbit it.

RADIUS A line extending from the center of a circle or sphere to its outer edge.

SPIN To turn around or rotate on a center point.

SUMERIANS People who lived in Sumer, one of the earliest known civilizations. Sumer started in southern Mesopotamia in about 4500 BCE.

FOR MORE INFORMATION

Books

Berne, Emma Carlson. *The Secrets of Mercury* (Planets). North Mankato, MN: Capstone Press, 2016.

Carson, Mary. *Far-Out Guide to Mercury.* New York, NY: Enslow Publishers, 2011.

Kazunas, Ariel. *Mercury* (21st Century Junior Library). Ann Arbor, MI: Cherry Lake Publishers, 2012.

Owen, Ruth. *Mercury.* New York, NY: Windmill Books, 2014.

Rhodes, Mary Wilson. *Journey to Mercury.* New York, NY: PowerKids Press, 2015.

Steinkraus, Kyla. *Rocky Planets: Mercury, Venus, Earth, and Mars* (Inside Outer Space). Vero Beach, FL: Rourke Educational Media, 2015.

Websites

Because of the changing nature of internet links, Rosen Publishing has developed an online list of websites related to the subject of this book. This site is updated regularly. Please use this link to access this list:

http://www.rosenlinks.com/PE/merc